MEDITATION MIND

Emily Maguire is a singer-songwriter, composer and multi-instrumentalist. She has practised Tibetan Buddhism since 1999 after being diagnosed with bipolar disorder.

For Emma,
with best wishes,
em

MEDITATION MIND

Emily Maguire

First published in 2018
by Emily Maguire

FIRST EDITION

ISBN 978 0 9566801 3 6

CONTENTS

With thanks to Melissa Viney for inspiring me
to write a poem a day.

I dedicate this book to my teacher
Lama Jampa Thaye.

Now

It's a habit to write
To breathe
To fish around
For the coin in the
Wishing well
I have only so many
Summers left
Should I not enjoy
The long grass
In the cemetery
Walk slowly
Down the road
Noticing the tiny
Flowers on the kerb
Here today
Gone tomorrow
Would I had
Such wisdom
As can lift the sky
Off its axis
Float a cloud
In a coffee cup
Say to you
The moment is now,
Now, now.

Caterpillars

There are caterpillars
In my mind
Thoughts that could
Turn into something
Beautiful, or just
Remain, eating cabbage
Leaves and waiting
For something to happen.

Walking On Air

What I would give
To see the world
Through your eyes
Emptiness no longer
An object of fear
But an everyday reality
That lets you glide
Through life
Like that kite you had
As a boy
Bright yellow and red
Diving through the
Clear blue sky
No fears, no hopes
No regrets
Nothing but the absence
Of those things
So long tying you down
Making you think
This ground is solid
And you're stuck upon it
When really your feet
Are walking on air.

Illusion

There's always reasons
To be afraid
But then why would
We do anything
If fear was always
Building brick walls
Around our hopes
And dreams
As if we ever could
Be kept safe like
A ship in a storm
Far out at sea
Find safe harbour
Drop the anchor
And wait for another
Day to dawn
So easy to say
So much harder
To do but it is all
Illusion, no ship
No storm, no sea
Just space and time
In a universe
Of mind.

Wild Horse

It's a simple thing
To sit still
On a cushion
Surrounded by silence
Apparently simple
To focus your attention
On the flow
Of your breath
To count 1, 2, 3
Up to 21
But that's when you realise
Your mind is like
A wild horse
Unfettered, unbiddable
Full of energy
However tired I am
My mind still races around
I watch it go
Waiting for the moment
When I can slip
A harness on
And lead it to water.

Words

Words are like windows
My heart is a house
I spend most of my time
Outside in the wind
Wondering why I'm always cold
I see faces but I don't
Recognise them, I don't see
My mother, again and again
The sublime in the ordinary
A jewel among stones
Only my preoccupation
With my wants, my needs
As if cutting down trees
Ever grew a forest.

Room

You had a room
And a window
On the world
A blanket on the bed
A door you could
Open, pills and
More pills, nurses
More nurses
And all that time
Unbeknownst to any
Of them
Words were pouring
Out of your head
Like blood from
A wound
Poured onto the page
Your fears, your hopes
The terror, the transformation
And here, safe
In my tower of sanity
I read and remember
My room, my window
All those pills and nurses
The beginning, middle
And end of it all.

Fire Burns

Why is it
That even though
I know that
Fire burns
I light a match
Anyway.

One Of These Days

Thoughts, feelings,
Fingers, toes
Who is this I
Some amorphous
Mass of me
I ascribe this identity
That has no truth
No existence
Like looking for
The moon in water
The sun in the sea
There is only the
Ever-changing
Dance of winds
And drops
And at the centre
Of it all
Space and time
And consciousness
The steady stream
That has no beginning
And no end
Life after life
After life after life
So after all my wrangling
My angst, my hopes
My fears, my dreams
There never was a me
There at all
Just illusions
No need to arm myself

When I've nothing to protect
No need to grasp at things
When I've nothing to gain
This is a castle
Without walls
Without moat
It floats upon the air
And yet there's nothing
There, and all I can say
For sure is this self
Is a figment of my
Imagination
A dream of desire
Hatred and ignorance
I would do well to
Wake up
One of these days.

Telepathic

Not being telepathic
I can't tell from your
Fingers what you're
Thinking, no trembling
Or tapping, or clenching
Hands on the wheel
I glance at your profile
But it remains
Sphinx-like, inscrutable
Like a statue
And I wonder what
Furious activity is going on
Beneath that skull
And if I'd be surprised
Or alarmed if I knew
Or whether you have
Mastered the art of
Emptiness and there's
No thought there at all
Beyond getting from
A to B as fast as possible.

Boulder

Looking forward
To the future
Is my main concern
While the days dance by
Am I supposed to be
Achieving something
Other than self-
Flagellating, self-
Aggrandising, any
Which way preoccupied
With self
I would rather
Roll a boulder
Over the mouth
Of my cave
Stay inside for an eon
Or two
At least till I'd learned
What a fool I've been
Thinking I was more
Important than you
That the future would be
Any different to the past
The same old party tricks
The same old games
We love to play over and over
Till the lights go out.

Just In Time

I could be clever
But much better
To be wise
To have eyes
That see the whole
Horizon
That can see the
Next wave coming
Just in time.

Saturn

Has Saturn shifted
Or the season changed
Or simply my mind
Effervescent as usual
Some obscurations cleared
Like fog on a summer's day
And suddenly the air
Is clear, bathed in
Sunlight, and I can see
I can breathe again
I know where I am going
Glad to be alive
Glad to have survived.

Tiger-Shooting

Go tiger-shooting
He said
Even though he
Could not speak
Act brave
Even when you
Don't feel it
And I thought
Is that what you did?
Clutching the map
In the back of the bomber
Wondering if this
Would be your last
Mission, your last flight
And here am I
Facing an audience
Of kind-hearted people
And feeling frightened
He must be laughing
Up in heaven.

The Only One

It's easy to put
One word
In front of the other
Less easy to walk
The wire
Every day a minefield
And I am on the edge
As usual
With everyone else
We are all anxious
All the time
To some degree
And I wish I'd known that
All those years
Thinking I was
The only one
Afraid.

Breeze

Silence is a sound
I'm used to
On my cushion
My thoughts
A quiet cacophony
But around me
Is stillness
No objects move
Nothing to be done
Bar breathing
And staying alive
For another 15 minutes
I can do that
I've had practice
And I've nothing much
To lose
Except my life
So solid, so fragile
Like a spider's web
Flickering in the breeze.

Butterflies

So things are not
How I want them to be
I can't arrange my life
Like butterflies
On a board
Colour-coordinated
Labelled, each static wing
Firmly in place
No chance then of
A maverick flight
That could bring down
An avalanche on the
Other side of the world
Bring all my best-laid plans
Crashing down around my ears.

Polar Bear

I could say it's an illusion
This polar bear
On my doorstep
I blink but there he is
Large, white
With big teeth
Really I should just
Shut the door
And he'd probably
Go away but there's
This fascination that
Goes with horror
Like crawling past
The car crash
On the motorway
Thinking at least
It's not me there
Mangled in metal
But now here's this
Polar bear on my
Doorstep and I know
He's not real but
I'm going to scream anyway
Just in case.

Precious Human Life

It's a funny thing
This busyness
However much I do
There's always more
To be done
I cross one thing
Off my list
And another appears
And I don't have time
To wonder
If any of it
Will be of any use
When my heart
Has stopped beating
When I've no more
Breaths to take
Or if all these things
Will turn out to be
A monumental
Waste of my
Precious human life.

Jump

Balanced on a point
Like a ballerina
One leg high in the air
About to make
An impossible leap
And I know
Don't you worry
That I could fall
Flat on my face
But I have something
Like faith in my heart
That the air
Will carry me
And all I need to do now
Is close my eyes
And jump.

You Wonder How

You wonder how
You survived
All those brick walls
All those brutal
Thoughts banging
Round your head
As if you'd been convicted
Ignorant of the crime
Punished all the same
But you are the jailer
And the prisoner
You hold the key
So tight inside your hand
And yet the door is there
The lock unturned
I wish I knew the answer
The words to set you free
Nothing makes sense
When you really look at it
Suddenly brick walls
Become windows
Feelings become air.

Right

I know
I should have gone
Right
But something
Turned my head
And before I knew it
My feet were walking
Left
And there's no-one
To blame
But me.

The Weight Of My Heart

When all's said
And done
It won't be gold
In my grave
To give the ferryman
I have nothing
In this world
But the weight
Of my heart
The bigger the better
And all that love
Will keep me warm
When the time comes.

Forever And A Day

You had big dreams
But you kept them
Locked up
In your head along
With the dark memories
And angry feelings
Did you design
Your life for
Disappointment
So you could say
I was right, it would
Never work out
It would all go wrong
In the end
Or was it less intended
More fate not being
On your side
The break that never
Came so now you're
Older, wise to this game
Of chance
That has no winners
In the end
And still hope like
A ray of light
Burns in your eye
So you keep going
Like the rest of us
We keep going
Because there's nothing
Else to be done

Sometimes winning
Sometimes losing
Always hoping the next
Roll of the dice
Will be a six
To fix our lives
Forever and a day.

Hills

If I could replace
Each negative thought
With a positive one
I would be radiant
Like a goddess
But as it is I am
Still human and that means
Full of worry, and
Much as I wish
I had your life
I'm sure if I was in
Your shoes I'd be
Looking at me
With something like envy
I wish I could
See it now, just a
Glimpse, see that
There is nothing to
Worry about, everything is
As okay as it will ever be
There is no mountain
To climb or raging torrent
To cross, just a winding
Path through the hills
Up and down.

Life Goes On

Waiting for an answer
As if the dark could speak
And I am holding
My breath like a diver
Who's run out of air
But doesn't want to
Surface quite yet
Wants to stay down
Deep down there
Beneath the waves
In the stillness where
Time is suspended
But life goes on.

Do You Slip Away

Do you slip away
Does it grow dark
Or light
Can you hear voices
Any sound at all
Do you feel cold
Do you feel anything
Can you see anything
Anything at all
Is there someone there
Anyone at all
Does it hurt
Are you detached
Are you on the ceiling
Are you in space
Do you remember anything
Do you remember
Your name
Do you feel sad
Or happy
Or do you not care
Either way
Are you on a road
Or in a cloud
Or a rainbow
Is it blank
Is there nothing
Or hallucinations
Of fire and water
Or emptiness
Peace?

Lap Of The Gods

I rest my head
In the lap of the gods
No way of knowing
If something is
Meant to be or simply
Chance, the luck of the draw
And I could be lying here
Some time, years even
Before getting up and
Walking away into
The future.

A Lesson In Illusion

A lesson in illusion
This life
My mind
A box of tricks
And I am the conjuror
And the audience
Gasping in amazement
Seeing things disappear
Reappear
All at the sleight
Of a hand
But somehow I've forgotten
I am the conjuror
That I know this is
A trick
And how it works
The rabbit in a hat
The coin behind the ear
I think it's all real
No magic at all
But my life
Passing by
In the blink of an eye.

Decision

Perhaps fate can be kind
Help you avoid
The pitfalls
Stumbling around
In the dark
Most of the time
Propelled forward by
Blind hope
When really the sensible
Thing to do
Would be to stand
Very still
Let the air around you
Settle, until the decision
Has been taken for you
And all you have to decide
Is to make the best of it.

Digging

I found a spade
And started digging
Cos digging is what
You do with a spade
And soon enough
I'd dug a great big hole
And I was in it
Couldn't see out
Couldn't climb up
The sides
And I never thought
I'd be one to dig
My own grave
Before it was my turn
To die but somehow
I'd found a spade
And started digging
Cos digging is what
You do with a spade
And now there's nothing
I can do except lie
Down, maybe cover
Myself with the dirt
To keep me warm
You understand
Not to bury me alive
Though who knows
What happens once
You're 6 feet under
And can't come up
For air.

Atom

Something about a whisper
And bare white walls
All the space and silence
You could need
To clear your eyes and ears
Of the mist and mud
We were only ever going
To see someday that
Time has something to teach us
A moment infinitely flexible
Like an atom expanding
To embrace the universe
All of us watching and
Waiting for the sky to fall.

Wake Up

I have seen this face
A thousand times before
And yet I don't recognise it
I see a smile
And I turn towards it
I see a frown
And I turn away
I have a hundred reasons
For being brave
A hundred reasons
To be scared
I know not what I do
My thoughts the
God of my world
Mind only an ocean
I am without sail
Without compass
I have never seen
A shore
And yet there are dolphins
And sunsets
Moments of hope
Like huge waves
That crash me down
To the depths once more
And this is a dream
I've been dreaming
Since beginningless time
Life after life after life
Waiting for the moment
When I'll wake up.

Seed

These thoughts
Are like signs
In the sand dunes
Telling me which
Way is water
And I am close
To the oasis
I can almost
Smell the green
Time to trust
To plant another
Thought like a seed
In my mind.

Alice

From one hole
To another
You would climb out
Smell the wildflowers
For a moment
Then back down
Like Alice and her rabbit
The earth smelling
Of last night's rain
The sky a circle of blue
Above your head
As another dream begins.

Cushion

I sit on my cushion
Full of good intentions
Before my mind
Starts to wander
And I realise a
Hundred times
I'm lost in thought
My lips move to the
Sound of the mantra
But my eyes are unfocused
And my mind is
Somewhere else entirely
Every day I do this
Practice makes perfect
Or makes a habit
Out of distraction
Of not being rooted
In the present moment
The point at which
Something could change.

Storm

Funny how
When you stop fighting
The war ends
And you're wondering
Why it ever began
And if peace
Could be permanent
A habit of mind
We hardly notice
Until we're provoked
And suddenly
All the world's a storm
And you're the captain
Of a ship
A hundred lives
Depend on you
And of all the thoughts
Crashing through
Your head
Just one might be
Do nothing
Hold on to yourself
This too will pass.

Such Love As This

Schizophrenia
Some would say
The Holy Spirit
You say
And who am I
To argue
When such love
As this is
Pouring from
Your eyes
To make you sane
Would that disappear
Dead inside again?

Sunday Morning

Perhaps it's a little part
A few cells
Deep in the heart
Of my brain
Nothing more than
Neurons or electrons
Or whatever
Firing off at all angles
Some neuroscientist
Could probably explain
Why it is I wake
With my heart
In my mouth
As if the fire alarm
Had gone off
And not simply
That it's Sunday
Morning, again.

Enough

How many people
In all the world
Are calm and content?
Not worrying about
What happened
Or did not happen
About what they have
Or have not
To have everything
You need and
Everything you want
Even if that means
Hardly anything
At all
Richer by far than
The wealthiest worrier
Addicted to wanting
More when more
Is never quite enough.

The Secret

Feeling good
Is not a bad thing
In moderation
Of course
An air balloon
As opposed to a
Rocket
It's the letting go
Of the good things
That's as hard as
Letting go of the bad
My hands grasp
At the air
All those turrets
And dungeons
Never there
In the first place
But my heart
Breathes in fresh air
From the open window
See, it says
The secret is simple
Happiness you can only
Get by giving it to others.

If This Is A Dream

Time has no sides
No beginning
No end
Only now
And yet my mind
Is anywhere
But now
It's down a ravine
Sitting pretty on a cloud
Making rain fall
And sun rise
Without any concern
Of how I might feel
This mind of mine
As if a river
Would care about
Its rocks
The sea about
Its shore
The point is
I guess
If this is a dream
Then I am asleep
What on earth
Would I see
If I ever woke up?

Knots

There is an art
To doing nothing
I haven't quite
Grasped
Always something
I could be doing
Right now
Instead of staring
Out the window
Reading a book
Lying still
On the sofa
Watching TV
All the time
My mind
Like a spindle
Of thread
Unwinding
Unwinding
All those knots
Untied, relaxed
As if all the world
Had stopped
For a moment
And nobody
Died.

Climb And Fall

Do reasons
Make us reasonable
The whys and
Wherefores excuse
Our deadliest thoughts
Look down deep enough
To see how far
You've come
And somehow we've
Managed to erase
The whens and hows
All the infinite
Intricacies of causes
And conditions
Like seeds and
Stones we leave
Scattered behind us
As we climb and
Fall and climb
And fall, only
Seeing that circle
Of light, the promise
Of an end in sight
The answer to our prayers.

A Lifetime

Writing down the past
Memories become words
Moments gone
Like raindrops
Hitting the ground
You were wearing
A black top
That's easy to remember
As that's all
You ever wore
And I was looking
In your eyes
Trying to hold
Your gaze
Your attention
As if a lifetime
Could be enough
For this love.

To Be Wiser

Each moment an opportunity
To do something different
To go the road less travelled
To smile instead of cry
What would happen if I
Turned left instead of right
Walked up instead of down
The universe would adjust
Shift for a second
Enough for my mind
To open just a chink
To blink for one second
And I could see the endless
Possibilities of action and
Interaction - what would make
Me better, or worse,
To be wiser in other words.

Different

Moving molecules around
Rearranging the stars
Could I make your life
Different?

Supermarket

Is happiness
A state of mind
Or a way
Of being
Bobbing on the waves
Instead of flailing
Your arms
I can't stop
Things arising
But who am I
To say this is
Pleasant, that is
Unpleasant
I want this
I don't want that
As if I were in
Some gigantic
Supermarket
Picking my life
Off the shelves.

Smoke

Shape-shifting
Solid as a rock
Then soft like smoke
Wrapped around
My fingertips
This is my shadow
That turns my
Beaten heart
Into a lump of coal
Saying 'You, you, you'
Till my ears
Are ringing
With the sound of myself
My eyes have turned
Inside out
To gaze upon
My beautiful blood
And guts
And all the Buddhas
Of the western world
Cannot save me now.

Black Heart

This is my black heart.
Feel free to break it.

The Road To Heaven

Start where you are
She says
No matter how deep the hole
How high the walls
How narrow the ledge
How wide the desert
Start where you are
Angry, jealous, hurt
Hell is a good place to start
On the road to heaven.

Wait For The Stars

Easy to say
Hard to do
The story of
My life so far
Courage comes
From adversity
And that's a
Good thing
But sometimes
I wish I could
Pass on the
Adverse bit
And get to the
Green hills
Before it gets
Dark preferably
I would pitch
My tent and wait
For the stars.

Sunset

So simple it seems
In beautiful words
Laid out on the page
How to think
How to speak
How to act
Happiness is not some
Existential matrix
It is a simple formula
$A + B = C$
Make others happy
Treat them as yourself
Their needs first
Be cheerful, be light
Let feelings come and go
They are transient
As clouds, as waves
On a sea,
No need to drown in them
Just sit on the shore
And admire the sunset
When it comes.

The Lighthouse

I had fear in my heart
At first
My own head on the line
But then
I began to think it's not
Just me
It's you, and you, and you
We are all fighting
The same war
We are all on the losing side
If hope is your drug
It is also mine
Then in all that darkness
A light appeared
And I began to walk towards it
Like a ship at sea
Sees the lighthouse on the horizon
And knows help is at hand
You can find refuge
From this storm
We can all find refuge.

Train

I am tired
Of all this thinking
But my mind
Knows no other way
To be
There is no sleep
Without dreams
And perhaps no death
Without dreams either
This brain
The driver of this body
Until it runs out of steam
And its passenger
Alights at the station
Stares at the board
Finds another destination
Another train to ride.

Spectacles

I've had this thought
Before
Like a hazard light
Like an alarm
I know how to
Switch it off
But not how to
Stop it turning on
Anxiety a pair of
Spectacles
When I'm wearing them
Everything I see worries me
And I wish I could
Somehow take them off
Break the glass
With my foot
But I guess that's
Not my karma
Or fate whatever
You want to call it
No amount of wishing
Can drag the sun
From her bed
Can stop the rain
From falling
Only time
That great universal
Conjuror
Can pull the rabbit
Out of the hat

Make all my fears
Disappear once more.

Embracing

Instead of thinking
How can I change this
I'm thinking
How can I use this
And then I'm not pushing
Or pulling away
But embracing.

Pink

Such a small pill
A pink dot in my hand
Tames my fears
Makes me appear
To the world
Calm, collected
Is it a lie?
Am I really reeling
Inside?
Maybe I'm more together
Than I think
Maybe it's the fear
Of fear, the blanket
Covering the empty cage
The lion long gone.

Sarasvati

No words
Or none
Of any meaning
I wonder
What Sarasvati
Would say
About it
Would she be
Philosophical
Or a bit annoyed
That all this time
She is called upon
To bless
These inane scratchings
As if something
Divine could appear
Out of the mundane
A lotus from the mud
Perhaps
And maybe mud
Is a good metaphor
For my mind
Maybe I should
Think about
Planting some seeds
Or maybe I should
Stop thinking
So much
And start doing.
Now would be
A good time.

Table

This is a table
So they say
Pieces of wood
A few screws
Here and there
I use it as a table
But it cannot be
Defined as the sum
Of its parts
The sum is not a
Thing in and of
Itself, permanent
Autonomous, essence
Of table
Just like I cannot
Be defined as the sum
Of my mind and
Body, there is no
Me beyond these
Billion parts, all
Moving, all changing,
Inexorably, inevitably
Coming to an end.

Brains

Maybe it's something
I'm missing
A hole
In my head possibly
I could leave it alone
Or start poking
And prodding
Until my brains
Fall out
Onto the floor
What to do now?

Shore

It's no good
I suppose
Wanting to walk
Away from
The world
As if this were
A fairground ride
I could get off
Get my feet
On solid ground
Stop this spinning
Wishing I was
A tree or
A wave on the
Ocean, unthinking
Unfeeling, with
No concept
Of the future
No vision of
The past
Just the passing
Of time
Ruthless, relentless
Pounding my head
Against a careless
Shore.

So Many Things

So many things
Left to say
And only silence
Left to hear them
What was solid
Becomes a shadow
A space I can't fill
Don't go before I do
My heart would not
Withstand it
We may as well
Hold hands and
Jump together.

Water

Love is like water
It follows the path
Of least resistance
It can leak through
The smallest gap
It can be frozen
It can impale you
It makes everything
Impossibly alive
You can drink it
You can swim in it
You can drown.

Second By Second

In hindsight
It would seem
So obvious
No microscope
No telescope
Required
Really just to
Open my eyes
A chink
And not blink
For 7 seconds
And I would see it
Clear as day
Every cause
Every condition
And you there
A river of stars
Draining away
Second by second.

Transit

There are a million reasons
A million answers
But none make sense
Confronted by a truth
You have no way
Of denying
That some fly long
Some fall short
We are all in transit
Transient, clutching at
Straws, reaching for
Rainbows, and so there is
Nothing I can say
Except I'm sorry
And hold out my hand.

A Universe Called Mind

Just as I get used
To how things are
They change
Why be surprised
The tides have been
Turning since
Beginningless time
Their ceaseless rhythm
The crashing of wave
Upon rock
The ageless love
Between the shore
And the sea
And as for me
Speck of dust
In an endless desert
Why should my
Desires mean anything
Why should my fears
Hold any water
What if there is no me
Anyway, just the dust
The drop of water
And a universe called mind.

Wood For The Trees

Any place but here
Any moment but now
The constant striving
Towards a horizon
You can never reach
That does not exist
A mirage of the future
Give up all hope
And you will find happiness
Was right under your nose
Under the floor of your room
And you had been searching
The deserts and the hills
And the deep oceans
All along you were a Buddha
Perfect and complete
But you didn't realise it
Didn't see the wood for the trees.

Martyrs

It could just be one word
Followed by another
That changed the world
A moment of careless
Righteousness, a flick
Of a red button
And we'd all be toast
Wondering why we ever
Tried to run this world
That had our name on it
Entrusted to us by
A reckless God perhaps
Who wanted to see
What we would do
With the porcupines
And the rainforests
Surely not burn the
Ground beneath our feet
Like martyrs at the stake.

Hole

Sometimes I forget
The road I'm travelling on
Too busy looking left
Looking right
My feet unknowing
Tread random steps
And it's only chance
Or fate
That dictates whether
I'm still standing or
At the bottom
Of a very deep hole.

Sell-By Date

Are we born
With a sell-by date?
Pre-ordained
The arrow's flight
Short or long
Written in the stars
And no amount
Of praying and
Pills can change it
We all are
On the assembly line
Of life, knowing
But not knowing
Peaceful they said
I hope I will be
Peaceful too
And what extraordinary
Revelation to come
After all that wondering
To know what
Actually happens!

Seaweed

I could go on
And on
Reasons to be anxious
Like seaweed
On a shore
You only see at
Low tide
But it's always there
Ready to curl itself
Round your legs
As you try and swim
In shallow water
Make for deeper water
It can't grab you there
Instead another world
Of fish, shark and whale
Waiting beneath the waves.

Ocean

We're all bobbing
About on the same
Ocean
I'm on one wave
You're on another
Up down up
We go
These waves that
Will never see a
Shore
Just an island
In the distance
We never quite reach.

Everything Is Possible

You were waiting
For something to happen
As if fate was
Fighting your corner
And all you had to do
Was wait
Something in the air
Something in the water
No choices, no decisions
Just the big open spaces
Where anything could
Happen, and usually does
That sense of excitement,
Anticipation, like a dog
About to get its dinner
But you have no idea
What you'll be getting
And whether it will
Fill up that chasm
Beneath the concrete
Or leave you empty
Wondering why you
Never reached for the
Stars when all the time
They were out there
In space, waiting
For you to realise that
Everything is possible.

Waiting In The Wings

Doubt like a dagger
In my side
And it's all I can do
To stem the flow of
Blood, inspiration
Draining away
Leaving me white and
Lifeless, lost in the
Mundanity of everyday
Suffering, dissatisfaction,
Disappointment, the
Usual fare of human
Beings being unaware
Of the possibility of
Salvation, of heaven
Waiting in the wings
If we could only turn
And see it.

Being Brave

Being brave
Means being scared
Every cell
In your body
Saying run
As you turn
To face the future.

Candle

Will I ever wake
From this dream
Of angels and demons
Would they melt
Into mist if I did?
Would I see the trees
And the wood divisible
Yet interdependent
An infinite matrix
Of causes and conditions
And I am but one tiny
Black dot
On a vast canvas
Of space
And you are one star
In an infinite galaxy
Words not big enough
To contain the truth
Words not wise enough
To describe the way
Things really are
And me, atoms
Of space and time
Imagining I am a
Mothership when all
I really am is a
Flickering candle
Burning down, down.

Dust

I could tell myself
It doesn't matter
And in the grand
Scheme of things
Of course it is a
Dust mote in the air
But I will go to
My grave covered
In such dust as this
Wondering why
I cared so much
Why I couldn't just
Blow it away
While I was out
In the open air.

Bend

Sometimes you have the
Illusion you're on a
Straight road
You can see the horizon
In the distance
Which you know
You'll reach some day
And you think you
Can see this straight line
Taking you there
But then suddenly
There's a bend, and
Another, and there you are
Careering round the
Twists and turns of life
Trying to hold on to
Your seat, trying not
To crash, and either
Grateful or aghast
At what is happening
To you now.

Cliff

The wind is in my hair
Birds duck and dive
Around my head
My feet stand on
An edge
And I should know
This is a cliff
But somehow the urge
To take one more step
Overwhelms me
And it's not that
I think I can walk
On air
Or that I have wings
Somewhere beneath
This coat
But that I feel
Fate will carry me
Wherever I am
Supposed to go
And that is all
I need to know.

Hearts

It's a guessing game
Chance
We take our turn
To play a hand
Hoping it will work out
That we have not
Risked everything
On the ace of spades
When trumps were hearts.

Seagull

What thoughts
Has a seagull
Thirty miles
From the sea
Something's missing
Something's wrong
I'm not where
I ought to be
But we have
These thoughts
Every day
We are all
Missing something
I'd go back home
If I knew
Where home is
Not left wandering
Like a seagull
Missing the sea.

Coming Down

It looks good
From up here
Bright, breezy
Blue skies
Every day
And I know
It's not safe
Sitting on a cloud
But if you tried it
I'm sure you
Would agree
That it looks good
From up here
Coming down
To earth
With a bang
Or a whimper
Is just the price
You pay
For gravity.

Mountain

After all that
The angst
The trepidation
Relief somehow
Never the size
Of the mountain
Above you
That somehow
You climbed
And on reaching
The top
Saw another
Peak in front
Of you
Never-ending
Until you fall
Off the edge
Of the earth.

Long Way Down

All these words
Yet I have nothing
To say
No wisdom
No confession
As if silence
Was a sound
And I'm listening hard
Trying to make out
The whispers
In my ear
Maybe I can't
Hear them
Because I don't like
What they're telling
Me – that this
Is a slippery slope
And it's a long way down.

Diver

Take me outside
Don't shoot me yet
Open my mouth
Make me take
A breath of fresh air
Like a diver
Going down
Who doesn't know
If he'll see daylight
Again.

Up

Maybe there are
No words to say
Just the touch
Of hand on shoulder
Is enough to say
You care
Don't give up
Rock bottom
Means the only
Way is up.

Unbroken

Things we think
We'll never get over
Pass by and into
The distance
Like a giant wave
Till all that remains
Is a shell with
An echo of the sea
The tempestuous sea
That once swelled
And crashed and
Made you think
Your carefully constructed
Shore would be totally
Destroyed. And yet
Look here now, it is
As it is,
A little battered
But unbroken.

Gratitude

It's like
Not seeing the sun
For a hundred years
A flower with
Five petals
Still water
Reflecting the sky
I enjoy everything
As if for the first time
The crisp, cool air
The wizened leaves
The birds flying
All these things
A delight
A thought of gratitude
To be out
Of the darkness
Once more.

Begin Again

They say there's a part
Of your brain which
Remembers everything
I wonder if it knows
Where I put the scissors
Or what the name of
Your old cat was
I would like to remember
The sound of winter
The smell of spring
But it seems mother
Nature has forgotten
How to do the seasons
So the trees forget to
Shed their leaves
Roses bloom in December
Creatures are all awake
And busy being busy
And I am much like
I am every other time
Of the year - flawed,
Distracted, inspired,
Hopeful that the turning
Of the year will change
Things for the better
Without me having to
Do much my end of the
Bargain, just watch
And wait and begin again.

Tunnel

For a long time
There was just a tunnel
Then at some point
A light appeared
In the distance
And I kept walking
And it got larger
And I was fearful
Frightened it was
A train coming
To run me down
But then no train
Came and I walked
Out into daylight
Into the spring sunshine.

Start Walking

There's something
About doing
Nothing that seems
Impossible and yet
Necessary
If I'm to carry on
Make some kind
Of progress
Even walk a
Straight line
I need to measure
Out time
With an hourglass
Give me a day
An hour
To find some
Space around
My head
As if all this
Never happened
As if all this
Is meant to be
And I can clamber
Out the sides
Of this man-shaped
Hole, see a
New horizon
Button up my coat
And start walking.

A Year Older

A year older
A year closer
What have I learned?
That time is change
That time is as cruel
As it can be kind
That to move forward
I mustn't look back
To move up
I mustn't look down
Keep breathing
While you can
See the world
Through someone else's
Eyes.

Spring

Where did this spring
Come from?
All these words
Like water rushing
Down a mountain
And I worry that
The flow will cease
Dry up even though
Thoughts and feelings
Have no end
Maybe it's time
For something different
Water after all
Is a cycle
You can't rain forever
You'd run out of
Clouds and I'm only
Thinking of a pause,
Some time to let
Whatever this is
Regenerate, refill
Wait a while
See what it's like
To be a tree
Rooted, but bending
In the breeze.

The Door

The door is open
A chink
Just enough
To let some light in
Just enough
For me to see
The world
On the other side
Of this wall
And it's a place
Of opportunity
And fulfilment
Where flowers grow
And the air
Is clear
I could walk for miles
No more walls
Only gates
To go through
And beyond
To new horizons
New lands
Eyes wide
Heart open
As if this were
The very first time
I'd ever been born.

Gone

Knowing when
It's time
To move on
Is almost as
Important as
Knowing when
It's time
To stay
Patience always
Possible if I
Can still this
Restlessness
Quieten the voices
Whispering in
My ear
What are they saying?
Where do they come from?
Questions are many
Answers are few
And so I keep walking
And hope that the path
Is true
That someday
I will arrive somewhere
And be glad
That I had gone.

A New Day Dawning

All we see
Is beginnings
And endings
Ghosts in the water
Become ghouls on land
Or angels in the air
All the time
I'm telling myself
A story,
Once upon a time
I was born,
I lived, I still live
(Will always live
Like a fool I feel)
And so I sleep on
Tossing and turning
On the ocean of
Samsara, never
Comfortable, never
At ease for more
Than one second
Always another
Thought to blow me
This way or that
To lift me up
To throw me down
Everything seeming
So real I believe
It to be true
But I'm breathing
Solid air

That does not exist
Any more than the
Wind after the storm
Has passed
Than the clouds
In a clear sky
My mind so preoccupied
With wishing and wanting
I cannot see the mirror
Let alone the reflection
I could reach out
My fingers would touch
Glass, not my face
So what is real
Me, the mirror
The sky, the sea
The wind, the clouds
Nothing changes
Everything is different
My eyes have been
Turned inside out
They no longer see
Ghosts or ghouls
Or angels, all they
See is light
Clear light
And a new day
Dawning.

One Precious Moment

Now
Is a good moment
To start
No more than this
Enough
Whatever happens
Or does not
To dance
In the breeze
To wander through
These fields
And gullies
Curious but unafraid
As if each step
Was a mile
In itself
And you could cover
The world
With your feet
Watching the stars
Spin by
As your life unfolds
One precious moment
At a time.

An Infinite Mind

If I was wise
Then I could see
There is no you
And there is no me
All there is
In space and time
Is the love and grace
Of an infinite mind.

For songs, videos and Emily's story, please visit
www.emilymaguire.com